WHAT WOULD YOU SAY?

AN HONEST LOOK AT
HALF A HEART FOR GOD

KATRINA BAZZOLI

WHAT WOULD YOU SAY?

AN HONEST LOOK AT
HALF A HEART FOR GOD

Foreword by Tricia Carrier

To request permissions, contact author at
klittlepage93@gmail.com

Paperback: ISBN 978-1-66782-707-0
Ebook: ISBN 978-1-66782-708-7

First paperback edition January 2022.

Edited by Jennell Houts
Cover art by Eli Creasy.

Printed by BookBaby

BookBaby
7905 N. Crescent Blvd
Pennsauken, NJ 08110
https://store.bookbaby.com/

ACKNOWLEDGMENTS

To my husband, Easton.
Thank you for the continuous prayer, support, and encouragement throughout the process of writing this book. You were my constant soundboard, and I couldn't imagine doing it without you by my side. I love you!

To my dear friend, Tricia.
Thank you so much for all that you've done to contributing to my first book! You edited, encouraged, prayed, and so much more. I wouldn't have it any other way. Thank you so much!

To my sister, Carmen Aranda.
I love you! You're a huge part of the reason why this book is here. Your presence my senior year of college was a gift and I'm forever thankful for our friendship. Thank you for loving me well and challenging me to love Jesus more.

What Would You Say?
An Honest Look at Half a Heart for God

"In a culture that screams 'Live your truth!' I'm so incredibly encouraged by a young sister in the church who is earnestly and passionately seeking to understand, teach, and celebrate *God's* truth. Katrina's frequent, sound, and affectionate use of scripture will edify and build up believers of all ages, and will challenge those in a Bible-belt context who may claim Christ but have no real affection for Him in their hearts. Her narrator is humble and relatable, and I was continually reminded of the ways that God redeemed me out of my own sin and replaced my heart of stone with a heart of flesh. Read this book, buy it for students in your life, and be encouraged by it!"

Ted Kluck, two-time Christianity Today Book-of-the-Year winner, assistant professor of journalism at Union University

For those who are familiar with the life of Jesus, but have never truly studied the words of Jesus - pick up this book! Katrina offers a simple and compelling treatment of what it truly means to follow Jesus. Reading and applying these pages will lead to a fruit bearing life!

Ben Weber,
Director of Campus Outreach
Birmingham

Your book is phenomenal. Genuinely, I mean it from the bottom of my heart. As I read it, I couldn't help but to think about how important it is for fellow believers to be reminded of God's call to holiness. I also loved how you ask your audience questions within your book. This is so important. Doing so allows your reader to not simply read your book for information's sake, but to be self-reflective. Your questions are extremely pointed and require pausing. I am so encouraged!

Carine Lewis, Urban Hope
Community Church Women's Director

I am convicted, challenged, inspired, but also reminded of my purpose after reading the words on these pages. This book will grow your relationship deeper with Christ and help you understand the love of the Father and how He is waiting to accept you no matter the worldly decisions you have made in the past. Whether you are a new believer, have walked with Christ for many years now, or if you have yet to decide to accept Christ as your Lord and Savior, this book is for you. I have no doubt in my soul that by the end of this book, your life will be changed forever, for His glory and for your good. So, grab your highlighters and pens because you will want to take notes of everything God is saying to you through, *What Would You Say!*

Thank you for being faithful, my friend.

Ashley Minor, Fellowship of Christian Athletes Representative at The University of Texas.

TABLE OF CONTENTS

FOREWORD

If you're holding this book in your hand, then I invite you to grab a hot cup of coffee and snuggle up in your favorite cozy spot and join Katrina on a journey. It's a journey of self-reflection and honest assessment. She will make you pause and ponder as you read. The questions are so tenderly intentional that it may even make you wonder if she's sitting across from you with a cup of hot coffee in her hand too. This book is powerfully practical and sheds light on concepts that are too cloudy to comprehend or so commonplace that we have allowed ourselves to be too complacent with them.

I first met Katrina a few years ago and we became fast friends when we realized how much we both love people and the Word. My daddy would always tell me that God's Word and God's people last forever. Then he would challenge me with a direct question, "So what are you doing to invest in both?". Katrina is fully invested in both and as you read the words she has penned; I pray you will also feel seen and known by her even if you do not know her personally. Because if you did, you would know that she speaks truth from a deep well of love for you that is rooted in the Word.

Katrina also has a tendency to ask direct questions just like my daddy did. This book begins with a foundational question that changed the trajectory of Katrina's life. It could change yours as well if you take time to intentionally invest in the truth found throughout the pages of this book. Katrina has purposefully woven numerous Scripture into this masterpiece and unpacks the meaning of each verse in straightforward ways. This book is a primer for practically understanding parables taught by Jesus, poetic words by prophets, and preaching by the apostle Paul.

In a culture of chaos, this book will help you drown out the noise and focus directly on the questions of life that you want answered. Katrina is boldly and refreshingly vulnerable with her personal stories. Real is rare and this book is a treasure chest. If you're a teenager wondering what the meaning of life is or searching for truth, don't put this book down. Katrina will help you find your way. If you're a weathered veteran in the church but stagnant and weary from doing all the right things, keep reading. Katrina will encourage you to keep fighting the good fight. If you have never stepped foot in a church and know nothing about the Bible, this book is a great place to start. Katrina will be a wonderful guide to the heart of God no matter your age or stage of life.

Whatever the reason you have for picking up this book, I pray you will finish the journey with Katrina. It will be an investment of time well spent as you continue your journey with a whole heart for God. He is the Way, the Truth, and the Life and no one comes to the Father except through Him (John 14:6). Hallelujah what a Savior!

Tricia Carrier
Jackson, TN

INTRODUCTION

The worst thing a book can do for a Christian is to leave him with the impression that he has received from it anything really good; the best it can do is to point the way to the Good he is seeking. The function of a good book is to stand like a signpost directing the reader toward the Truth and the Life. That book serves best which early makes itself unnecessary, just as a signpost serves best after it is forgotten, after the traveler has arrived safely at his desired haven. The work of a good book is to incite the reader to moral action, to turn his eyes toward God and urge him forward. Beyond that it cannot go.

A.W. Tozer

"Why did you decide to write a book?"

You may not be asking that question, but I'm asking myself that question with each word I type. If you asked anyone who knew me in school if they thought I would ever write a book, I'm sure they would laugh in your face. I was not the most studious person, nor was I ever up for a new and difficult challenge. I was pretty satisfied with just getting by.

As a decent collegiate athlete, I was fine with my sport being my "thing." But God's sense of humor is humbling at times. I was not a writer at all in school. To be honest, I was very nervous about the degrees I chose because of how much writing I would probably have to do. I got my bachelor's degree in Sociology, which sounds like a lot of writing, but it wasn't as bad as I thought it would be. Soon after, I received my Master's in Education, which again, sounds like a lot, but it wasn't too bad. Somehow, I made it through two degrees without having to write a ton, and I praise God for that. But then, out of nowhere ... I had a small desire to begin writing.

I became a believer in Christ during my senior year of college (2016), and the urge to write about all things related to Jesus came about one year later. I wanted friends and family to see that the Word of God is still true and relevant in our lives today (Isaiah 40:6–8, I Peter 1:24–25).

I started writing what the Lord would lay on my heart as I read His Word; I just kept it to myself in a little blue journal. I definitely remember thinking, "God, I'm not sure what You want me to do with these writings, but hopefully not much." Typical me, just reminding God that my comfort was pretty important. Eventually I started to share my writings with others who encouraged me to continue.

When I began posting my writings on Facebook and Instagram, I thought, "There, God. I'm stepping out of my comfort zone and finally posting what You are laying on my heart." I did not want the possibility of someone telling me that they did not agree with me, that my writings did not make sense, or point out my grammatical issues. But I also felt that God wanted me to do more than just send it to a handful of people.

A few months later, a friend of mine told me that he had a dream about my writing a book. I literally laughed out loud, then changed the topic. Unbelievably, a few weeks later a professor asked me, "Do you ever plan on writing a book?" Similar scenarios continued happening up to this point, so now I'm writing a book!

Several people who loved the Lord and had a great relationship with Him encouraged me to write a book. And each time I thought, *unless I have a moment similar to Paul on the road to Damascus, I AM NOT DOING IT.* While I sat, waiting on God to tell me that He wanted me to write a book, I ignored every person He sent my way. Then, being as smart as I am (sarcasm!), I decided to start a blog. Books and blogs both have words and start with the letter *B* ... so there really isn't a huge difference, right?

I love blogging, and it's a lot of fun, but God kept reminding me that it wasn't quite what He was telling me to do. It helped quiet the nudge for a little while, but it did not last long. The blog is great, and I actually really enjoy doing it, but I couldn't get this frustrating quote out of my head: "Delayed obedience is disobedience."

For example, when I was younger, and my mom or dad told me to clean my room, I would not dare say, "I will do it later." Although I was saying I would do it eventually, it would have been disrespectful. And honestly, my parents would have "encouraged" my obedience with a belt to my butt—and quick! So, what was the difference here? I simply acted as if I did not hear God telling me what to do. If mom or dad told me to clean my room, and I "didn't hear them," then I should be fine because I didn't know, right?

The reason I started to write in my journal and then my blog is the same reason I'm writing this book: I want others to see that the Word of God is true, no matter the year, culture, or location; I also want to help people grow in why they believe what they believe.

I used to say I was a Christian way before I actually was one because it was the easy thing to do. Live a "good" life and claim Christ in the process. I did not realize that offering my best deeds to a Holy God was like giving Him filthy rags (Isaiah 64:6). If someone were to ask me why I was a Christian or to explain my beliefs to them, I would have struggled badly. I had no clue what it truly meant to love Christ with all your heart, mind, soul, and strength (Mark 12:30).

I pray that if you are already a follower of Jesus that this book will help you grow deeper in your faith. I want you to be able to adequately express what it means to be a follower of Christ in both word and deed. If you aren't a follower of Jesus, I'm happy that you've grabbed this book and pray that as you read along, you will discover how wonderful Jesus is and how much He loves you.

We live in a day where truth is no longer absolute. Everyone has their "own truth," but at our cores, we know that cannot be right. I pray that the words in this book challenge your heart and give you a desire to really dig for truth. During that dig for truth, you will find Jesus. He is the One who did not know sin to be sin for you and for me, so that "we might become the righteousness of God" in Him (II Corinthians 5:21, NIV). Amen.

CHAPTER 1:

WHAT WOULD YOU SAY?

"What would you say if you died tomorrow and were standing in front of God, and He said, 'Why should I let you into Heaven?'"

This question caught me off guard because I had never considered it before. I remember instantly starting to sweat a little, and my heart began to race. A little backstory of how and why I was asked this question in the first place will help you understand why I felt so uneasy.

I started meeting with a new friend, Carmen, who was a follower of Jesus. I also would have said I was a follower of Jesus, but after a few times of meeting with Carmen, I quickly realized there was a difference between us. God was starting to convict me of my lifestyle of sin, but I really did not want to let go of that lifestyle just yet. I would meet with Carmen once a week if our schedules allowed and ask questions about all things Christianity. Our topics ranged from heaven, hell, prayer, morality, and sexuality to name a few.

Soon after all these discussions, I wanted to talk about alcohol. Carmen suggested that we talk with Ben who was the director of the campus ministry that we attended because he would be able to give me more insight on the topic. I didn't drink alcohol in a way that affected my grades, my commitment to basketball, or my relationships with others, so I did not want to let that go. I was simply having fun.

I was creating a list of things that I would and wouldn't submit to God, and I did not understand what the big deal about alcohol was and why God did not want me getting drunk if I was responsible. I grew up seeing people act one way on Sundays and a different way on the other days of the week. The most important thing to me was the perception of myself that I gave off to others, not having a true relationship with God.

So, back to the question: "If you died today, why should God let you into heaven?" I said I was a follower of Christ at the time, but what I professed and the lifestyle that I lived didn't match up with what Christ taught. I believed that as long as I was a good person, I should get into heaven. Although I lied, got drunk often, was sexually impure, and never spent time with Jesus, I did "good" things like post inspiring Scriptures on Snapchat—feel-good verses like John 3:16 or Proverbs 3:5–6—not convicting verses like Revelation 3:16 nor Titus 1:16. I had intentional conversations with people and truly tried not to be "too bad" of a person. But what I failed to realize is that what I called "good" was like filthy rags to a *perfect, righteous, and holy God*. Isaiah 64 puts it this way:

How can we be saved if we remain in our sins? All of us have become like something unclean and all our righteous acts are like a polluted garment; all of us wither like a leaf and our iniquities carry us away like the wind (vv. 5b–6, CSB).

I believed that I could live a sinful life and that God was pleased with me because I was posting Scripture to make myself look good. And I was very wrong.

A True Disciple

What does it truly look like to follow Christ? Well, I John 1:6 tells us that if we say we have a relationship with God while walking in darkness, we lie and do not practice the truth. Romans 2:13 says it is not the *hearers* of the law who are righteous before God, but the *doers* of the law who will be justified. James 4:4 tells us that friendship with the world makes us an enemy of God. Ephesians 4:22 (ESV) says "to put off your old self, which belongs to your former manner of life and is corrupt through deceitful desires." The list goes on and on explaining how you can't be touched by Jesus without your life also being transformed.

I was living my life identical the rich young ruler (whom we'll call Richie) in Luke 18:18–23. When he met Jesus, he asked, "What must *I do* to inherit eternal life?" (Luke 18:18, CSB, emphasis mine). Richie believed that his goodness made him worthy of heaven. Do our actions in this life matter? Absolutely! Can they save our souls? Absolutely not. Jesus responded to Richie by revealing to him what he was holding onto while trying to earn his salvation. Jesus said, "You know the commandments: Do not commit adultery; do not murder; do not steal; do not bear false witness; honor your father and mother." I'm sure as Jesus was going through that list, Richie was thinking, *check ... check ... I've done all these things. What else?* That is when Jesus revealed a blind spot in Richie's life: "You still lack one thing: Sell all you have and distribute it to the poor, and you will have treasure in heaven. Then come, follow me" (Luke 18:22, CSB). The very next verse tells us that Richie became very sad, for he was extremely rich. Although Richie had done a lot of good things, his riches prevented him from seeing who Jesus really was. What "riches" are you holding onto that are preventing you from fully submitting to the Father?

"If you died today, why should God let you into heaven?"

My answer reflected my heart. I was no different than Richie. "I have done so many good things ... ," but I failed to mention the life, death, and resurrection of Jesus. That's when I realized that I had it wrong the entire time. I tagged on Christ, but I had no idea what that really meant. I then started to realize that my life could either look like Richie's or like Zacchaeus's. In the very next chapter of Luke, Jesus encounters another rich man whose response was very different from Richie's. Zacchaeus was a tax collector, which means he stole from people, and society deemed him a sinner. When Zacchaeus encountered the Person and Presence of Jesus, he opened both hands and fully grabbed ahold of Him.

> Behold, Lord, the half of my goods I give to the poor. And
> if I have defrauded anyone of anything, I restore it fourfold
> (Luke 19:8, ESV).

We see two very different responses from Richie and Zacchaeus. Richie, who has put a lot of faith in himself and has been a "good person" his whole life, had a checklist, and he was fine with getting the job done on his own. He only wanted Jesus for the gift of eternal life, but not for Jesus Himself. He wanted Jesus to be the Savior of his soul, but not the Lord of his life. There is a big difference between wanting the Giver Himself and wanting the good gifts the Giver can give.

Paul David Tripp says it perfectly: "Here is the spiritual reality that you need to know, understand, and live in light of— if you love the gifts and not the Giver, your heart will never be satisfied, but if you love the Giver, your heart will be content, and you will be able to enjoy His gifts while keeping them in their proper place." Richie enjoyed his gifts so much that whenever Jesus told him to let go of them, he chose the gifts instead.

Zacchaeus, on the other hand, was not there for what Jesus could offer him—he was there for Jesus Himself. He didn't expect a ten-step guide to eternal life or a lesson about things he could do to make his life better; he simply wanted a relationship with Jesus Christ. Zacchaeus did not try to hold onto some parts of his life and submit other parts; instead, he held both hands open and gave everything to Christ.

Back to the Question

"If you died today, why should God let you in?"

If you are really honest with yourself, how would you answer this question? Are you currently convinced that you can do enough "good" to earn your way into heaven? At the end of this life there are only two options that can happen:

First, God can see all your good works, but they will be accompanied by all of your bad as well. According to Matthew 7:21–23,

11

there will be people who believe that they should be in the presence of God, but they will be turned away: "Lord, Lord, didn't we prophesy in Your name, drive out demons in Your name, and do many miracles in Your name? Then I [Jesus] will announce to them, 'I never knew you! Depart from me, you lawbreakers'" (Matthew 7:22–23, CSB).

Second, God sees Jesus, not you. He doesn't see the good or bad things that you have done. Instead, God sees Jesus and Jesus alone. So, we have a choice. I encourage you to open both hands and allow Him to have every part of your life—not only the parts that you are okay with letting go of, but also the parts that you are gripping too tightly.

CHAPTER 2:
LIVE YOUR TRUTH

If you are on social media at all, you have probably seen or heard the term, "Live Your Truth." If you haven't heard that term, then surely you have heard the term, "Follow Your Heart." Usually, the context behind these terms is to encourage you to do whatever it is that makes you happy—you define yourself, and your feelings are more important than absolute truth. We are living in a time where truth isn't the driving force of decision-making, and how we shape our lives is based on our fluctuating feelings. Subjectivity is the new objectivity, confusion is the new clarity, and our feelings are now our god. So ... what is truth?

How Did We Get Here?

First, I think it is best to talk about the post-truth world we live in and how we got here. Before we got here, we dealt with postmodernism. Postmodernism denied the existence of any ultimate principles and rejected that scientific, philosophical, or religious truth could explain everything for everybody. It eventually started to die out in the 1960s, then post-truth started to rise in the early 1990s.

13

The definition of post-truth is: relating to or denoting circumstances in which objective facts are less influential in shaping public opinion than appeals to emotional and personal belief.[1] In other words, post-truth does not reject truth altogether but subordinates it while elevating feelings and preferences.

Abdu Murray, who is an apologist that I enjoy learning from said this: "A skeptic doesn't believe until there is enough evidence. A cynic doesn't believe even with evidence."[2] I pray that you do not fall into the trap of being a cynic and that you are digging to find the truth.

Objective truth is unbiased. That means that no matter what *I* believe about the claim, my opinion doesn't change that truth. For example, even if I believe with *all my heart* that the sun is cold, it is not. What *I* believe about the sun doesn't affect what is actually true about the sun.

Subjective truth, on the other hand, is a "truth" based on a person's perspective, feelings, or opinions. If *anything* can be truth, is it actually true? If everyone should live by "their truth," when is anyone ever considered wrong? If someone's truth is solely based on how they feel, then no one should ever be able to say what they are doing is right or wrong.

At first, you are probably thinking, *For sure! Exactly. People should be able to live the life they want to live, and no one should be able to tell them otherwise.* However, what if someone's truth is immoral? What if their "truth" is pedophilia (which, I'm not sure if you've read the news lately, but there are people who are trying to normalize and accept pedophilia)? Are we then still saying, "Live your truth"? Where is the line of someone being able or not being able to live "their truth"? These phrases are not only dangerous but also

14

a contradiction. This ideology is built on sinking sand, and it is not just in the world—it is creeping into the church as well. Believers are hearing motivational speeches from the pulpit instead of biblical truth, and we are forgetting that the Gospel is not about us. The only truth that matters in this world is *the One who is the truth.*

Whose "Truth" Will You Choose?

The world tells us to follow our hearts, but Jeremiah 17:9 (ESV) says, "The heart is deceitful above all things, and desperately sick; who can understand it?" The Bible tells us in many different ways that the Spirit leads us to life and truth, while the flesh, our heart, and passions will lead us to death.

> For those who live according to the flesh think about the things of the flesh, but those who live according to the Spirit, about the things of the Spirit. For the mind-set of the flesh is death, but the mind-set of the Spirit is life & peace (Romans 8:5–6, HCSB).

> I say then, walk by the Spirit and you will not carry out the desire of the flesh. For the flesh desires what is against the Spirit, and the Spirit desires what is against the flesh; these are opposed to each other, so that you don't do what you want (Galatians 5:16–17, HCSB).

> Dear friends, I urge you ... to abstain from fleshly desires that war against you (I Peter 2:11, HCSB).

> The one who trusts in himself is a fool, but one who walks in wisdom will be safe (Proverbs 28:26, CSB).

These are just a few verses, but the Bible is very clear from the Old Testament to the New Testament that "living your truth" and even "following your heart" puts you on a path that leads to destruction. Before Jesus was crucified, He told the disciples that He is the way, the **truth**, and the life (John 14:6). What does that even mean when Jesus says that He is "the truth"? It means that anything else contrary to Him is false. In our culture, this sounds like a harsh statement because everyone's truth is deemed "valid." People ask, "How could Jesus be the only way?" Either Jesus is who He says He is (Alpha and Omega, Lion and the Lamb, God in the Flesh, Just Judge, Holy Creator of everything) ... or He is not. It is either true ... or it is false.

Our flesh and society will continue to tell us to do what is pleasing, indulge in whatever makes you feel good, and live for today; but everything we do has eternal purpose. We often say, "Life is short," which is something we could probably all agree on. The Bible says that we are like a vapor in the air that is here today and then vanishes (James 4:14). So, what are we doing to invest in eternity? Living our truth with a little bit of Jesus is not following Jesus. That is following an ideal of Jesus that we can tolerate. If you are honest with yourself, whose truth are you living for?

CHAPTER 3:

"DID GOD REALLY SAY?"

Now the serpent was the most cunning of all the wild animals that the Lord God had made. He said to the woman, "Did God really say, 'You can't eat from any tree in the garden?'"
(Genesis 3:1, csb).

It's important to know how we got to this point in humanity, and it is vital to know how God intended things to be. So, let's start at the beginning—the *very* beginning. God makes literally everything in Genesis 1. He then goes on to create Adam in His image from the dust of the earth. God planted a garden in Eden and placed Adam there so he could work and watch over it.

Before God gives Adam his wife, Eve, He tells Adam, "You are free to eat from any tree of the garden, but you must not eat from the tree of the knowledge of good and evil, for on the day you eat from it, you will certainly die" (Genesis 2:16–17, csb). This was an important command from God right before He decides that it isn't good for man to be alone.

Adam and Eve's relationship with God before the fall was a beautiful picture of what our lives were meant to be. There was no shame, strife, or bitterness; instead, humans enjoyed each other, God, and His creation. The Bible isn't specific about how long time passed before Adam and Eve sinned, but it is often assumed that it wasn't too long. What we do know for sure is that the enemy was there and present in the beginning, and his aim has always been to deceive. Unfortunately, it wasn't long before Adam and Eve chose their feelings over what they knew to be true.

"Did God really say?" is a question that not only caused Eve to doubt God, but it is also the same question that causes us to doubt God today. Just to put this in perspective, Eve did not have hundreds of different beliefs coming at her all at the same time the way we do, but she did have Satan questioning her about the character of God. The serpent planted a seed of doubt in Eve's mind to question the commandment of God, making God's Word subject to human judgment. We were never meant to decide if God's Word is true or best, but it is the truth and best because of who He is. She was convinced that what God said was best for her was not true. While Satan still does the same thing to us today, we also have friends, family members, influencers, and others doing the same thing. How did we get here?

After Eve responds to the serpent, notice that Eve's response did not even match what God initially said. What God actually said was, "You are free to eat from any tree of the garden, but you must not eat from the tree of the knowledge of good and evil, for on the day you eat from it, you will certainly die" (Genesis 2:16–17, CSB). But what Eve says to the serpent is a little different. Eve's response was, "We may eat the fruit from the trees in the garden. But about the fruit of the tree in the middle of the garden, God said, 'You must not eat it or touch it, or you will die'" (Genesis 3:2–3, csb).

Knowing God's Word

The first problem we have is that Eve does not seem to know what God actually said herself. There is no way we can fight off the enemy with the Word of God if we do not know it ourselves. You may be thinking, *What is the big deal? She added one little thing.* But there are many dangers in adding to what God has actually said. You may even be even thinking that she could have been setting boundaries so she wouldn't be tempted to eat the fruit. Maybe! Maybe Eve thought that although God said not to eat it, she decided she wasn't going to even touch it.

I am totally for setting boundaries because it is intentional, wise, and even biblical; but adding them onto God's Word and saying that they are His boundaries is not the answer. We have seen people add to God's Word and live, teach, and lead others to live in a way that God never intended nor approved.

For example, the Book of Mormon is supposedly another testament of Jesus Christ—in other words, added words to the already finished Word of Christ. In II Nephi 25:23 it reads "... for we know that it is by grace we are saved, after all that we can do," while Ephesians 2:8–9 (csb) says, "For you are saved by grace, through faith, and this is not from yourselves; it is God's gift—not from works, so that no one can boast." Although the Book of Mormon only added a few words to that verse, they completely change what God actually said. Changing what God said can cause one to follow a god who cannot save.

Secondly, the heart of the issue comes to light in the garden: **You can be just like God.** We see that Eve is attracted to the thought of being equal to the One who created her. When the serpent deceived Eve into believing that she could be like God and knowledgeable about everything, he didn't mention what that would actually mean … nor what it would cost her. God knowing good and evil is a bit different than man knowing good and evil. Jackie Hill Perry says it like this:

> God has never known evil experientially, He only knows goodness that way. He knows evil like a doctor knows cancer. Something that He understands fully, but something that he has not dealt with Himself. But when Eve disobeyed the commandment of God, she did not get to know evil like the doctor knows cancer, she became the patient that knows cancer. She would become the one who was sick. In her deception, she didn't realize that sinning against God, she would become inherently unlike God.[3]

Eve, who only knew goodness, now knew evil in a way that God Himself didn't even know. Although Adam and Eve had a perfect relationship with God, the desire to know all ultimately prevailed over the truth that God had spoken to them. Eve was the first, but she surely was not the last who wanted to be like God.

We live in this "Live Your Truth" culture for the same reason today. The appeal of being like God—running the show, doing things our way—started in the garden and continues right here and now. This isn't just a worldly problem, but it is also something we are starting to see from professing Christians as well.

My Story

Before giving my life to Christ, I would have said that I was a believer, although my life looked more worldly than like a reflection of who I said I was following. I went to church on Sunday (sometimes), but there was no sustaining fruit throughout the week. For example, I went to a junior college my first two years for basketball before transferring to a university to play there. I was in a small town in Mississippi that didn't have a lot of options, but there was a church that I loved to go to. Remember, at this point in my life, I believed I was a good person, and that church was just basically motivation for the rest of the week. Obviously, the whole church thing was not a huge priority to me.

This church had one service, and it was at 8 a.m. If I had too much to drink Saturday night, you could count on my sleeping in and trying again next week. Although I said I was a believer, I got drunk often and then headed to Fellowship of Christian Athletes (FCA) since I was a "leader" there. Hypocrisy at its finest! I gave the parts of my life to Christ that I was okay with Him having and continued to hold onto the areas that I thought I could handle better than God.

In which areas of your life are you struggling to see God for who He is? We can only fight off the enemy and world with the truth, but we must know and believe that truth ourselves *first*.

CHAPTER 4:

LUKEWARM

I know your works, that you are neither cold nor hot. I wish that you were either cold or hot. So, because you are lukewarm, and neither hot nor cold, I am going to vomit you out of my mouth. For you say, 'I am rich, I have prospered, and I need nothing,' and you don't realize that you are wretched, pitiful, poor, blind, and naked.

(Revelation 3:15–17, CSB)

I'm not sure where you are from or where you are located, but in the Bible Belt, nearly everyone calls themselves a follower of Jesus Christ. You may even be one of those people. Like me, maybe you associated your goodness with following Jesus because that is what is taught: if you are a good person, you are a Christian. The problem is, when our works are what matter most, and we add a little Jesus to that, we are completely changing Jesus's final words on the cross, "It is finished" (John 19:30). Oftentimes, we compare ourselves to someone who is "not as bad" as we are, but we also make sure not to compare ourselves to someone "way better" than we are. In reality, our own sinfulness is real. No matter who we compare ourselves to, we are not good.

I'll give you a couple of examples. My husband, Easton, is quite tall— he is actually 6'6". When he played middle school basketball, he was easily the best guy in his area. He was more skilled, taller, and more athletic than most guys he played against. Since he compared himself to people who weren't as good, he assumed he would get a basketball scholarship to Duke—the Blue Devils Duke. Once Easton went and played against a few more skilled players, he quickly realized that he was not as good as he thought he was. Spoiler alert, my hubby did not go to Duke University (which is good because we probably would not have met if he did).

For me personally, I mentioned earlier about my love for alcohol before I was a believer. Growing up, I watched my mom struggle with alcohol a lot, and I remember thinking, "I'll be better. I won't be like that." Then my first year of college included a lot of alcohol, but I would have said I was "drinking responsibly." What I mean by that is, I got drunk and made sure I didn't drive, didn't miss class, didn't to show up hung over to any event, and didn't miss basketball practice. At the same time, I was giving my testimony at FCA and claiming to be a believer.

I compared myself to my mother instead of Jesus.

When we compare ourselves to other sinful people, we either feel really good about ourselves and then our lives are crushed whenever we meet someone better, or we become prideful and think that we are the example for everyone else. I boldly said I was a believer, but I believed that I had prospered and needed nothing (Revelation 3:17).

Lukewarm Believers

How does God feel about lukewarm believers? If you are a coffee drinker, you probably feel the same way I do about lukewarm coffee: once my hot coffee starts to get lukewarm, most likely I'm tossing it. In Revelation 3, God says the same about lukewarm believers to the Church of Laodicea. Personally, Revelation is a book that I tend to shy away from, and maybe you can relate. So here is a little context: the Letters to the Seven Churches in the book of Revelation (chapters 2 and 3) are believed to be letters providing lessons for all churches, no matter the time period. Laodicea was a wealthy city in Asia Minor. It was located on one of the great Asian trade routes which insured its commercial property, and it was also home to many wealthy residents (keep in mind how this relates to us in America).

Jesus addresses the church in Revelation 3:15–17 (csb) by saying,

> I know your works, that you are neither cold nor hot. I wish that you were either cold or hot. So, because you are lukewarm, and neither hot nor cold, I am going to vomit you out of my mouth. For you say, 'I am rich, I have prospered, and I need nothing,' and you don't realize that you are wretched, pitiable, poor, blind, and naked.

Harsh and vivid words there, right? The problem was not simply the lives that they lived but who they said they belonged to while living that life. God was confronting them because in front of the "church" crowd, they had all the right things to say and displayed passion for the Lord, but in front of others they acted as if He wasn't that important.

Also notice that in these verses, Jesus isn't gently trying to convince the church to be on fire for Him, but He is very clear: you are either for Him, or you are not. The lukewarm lifestyle of a believer nauseates God. Clearly, He would prefer for our speech and deeds to line up with His Word instead of saying we believe, but our actions reveal that we don't. In short, saying we're a believer while living like the world dishonors God.

An example of the lukewarm Christian that I want to point out are false converts. One could be living the life of a lukewarm Christian simply because he or she is not actually a believer. First John 2:19 (CSB) says,

> They went out from us, but they did not belong to us; for if they had belonged to us, they would have remained with us. However, they went out so that it might be made clear that none of them belongs to us.

Maybe an experience or a feeling made you "commit" your life to Jesus. You may have responded to an altar call when you were younger or said the sinners' prayer, but there was never fruit from that commitment. Maybe you even heard that if you add Jesus to your life, you would get all of your wants and desires; you gave it a try, but in reality, it wasn't what you really signed up for.

If you truly give your heart to Jesus, transformation follows. Second Corinthians 5:17 (HCSB) says it like this: "Therefore, if anyone is in Christ, he is a new creation; old things have passed away, and look, new things have come." Once you truly see Jesus for who He is, you have a genuine joy and yearning to love Jesus more than you love any created thing. Once He captures your heart, the lifestyle that disappoints Jesus will also disappoint you.

Faith and Works

In one of the most misused verses (in my opinion), James tells us that faith without works is dead (James 2:17). Often, I see people use this verse to motivate one to accomplish a big dream they have always had. You have faith in this dream, now you need to work hard to make it happen. This verse has nothing to do with motivating you to do the work to accomplish your dream. James is telling the audience that you cannot say you have faith in the living God and not have works to prove that faith.

Imagine you are on an airplane, and the pilot announces, "Put on a parachute! The plane is going down, and you will need to jump." If you trust in the parachute, then you will jump. The faith that you have in the parachute to save you compels you to not only put on the parachute but to also jump because you trust it will save your life.

James gives the example of Abraham and Isaac to illustrate his point. In Genesis 22, God tells Abraham to sacrifice his one and only son Isaac. I can only imagine what Abraham was thinking and feeling in this moment. God, who had promised him a child for so long, was now telling Abraham to sacrifice that child. Abraham not only said "yes" to God in this moment, but his actions also followed that yes, proving his faith in God's Word and promise. (If you are unfamiliar with this story—spoiler alert—Isaac lives). Saving faith entails more than knowledge; it also includes trust and obedience. Because faith without works is dead.

Parable of the Two Sons

What do you think? A man had two sons. And he went to the
first and said, 'Son, go and work in the vineyard today.' And he
answered, 'I will not,' but afterward he changed his mind and
went. And he went to the other son and said the same. And he
answered, 'I go sir,' but did not go. Which of the two did the will of
his father?" They said, "The first." Jesus said to them, "Truly I say
to you, the tax collectors and the prostitutes go into the kingdom
of God before you. For John came to you in the way of righteous-
ness, and you did not believe him, but the tax collectors and the
prostitutes believed him. And even when you saw it, you did not
afterward change your minds and believe him.
(Matthew 21:28–32, ESV)

The Parable of the Two Sons is one that crosses my mind when I think of the lukewarm believer. For some context, Jesus is confronting the hypocrisy of the Pharisees. In the earlier verses of Matthew 21, the Pharisees are trying to challenge Jesus, but He only plans on giving them an answer if they can answer a question for Him first. Jesus asks a couple of questions: "Where did John's baptism come from? From heaven or from man?" (Matthew 21:25, HCSB). Answering the question with either of the answers contradicts everything they claimed to believe. If they answered that John was from heaven (or from God), then Jesus could point out how they ignored the messenger whom God sent, which would also show that they did not acknowledge Jesus for who He was. If they denied that John was sent by God, the crowd of people would pushback because they believed God sent John. No matter how they answered, it would reveal that they did not acknowledge Jesus's authority. Jesus asking those particular questions put the Pharisees in a position to look

28

like hypocrites no matter how they answered, so instead they did not answer at all.

Now that we understand the context, let's talk about the two sons. We notice that one of the sons says "yes" but does not actually go through to do the work of the father. Afterward, we see the son that says "no" but later changes his mind and goes to do the work. I can't help but think that the son that says "yes" is very similar to those who say "yes" to Jesus but then there is never an adoration or love for the Father. The "yes" came in a moment of guilt or maybe to just blend in with the crowd but never for a genuine desire to be in relationship with the Creator.

The Pharisees' "yes" stemmed from their bloodline. They were in the bloodline of Abraham, and they knew a lot about the Father, but their hearts were still hard. They looked down on everyone forgetting that they, too, were sinners in need of the grace of Jesus. Like the Pharisees, did your "yes" come from your bloodline? Your "goodness"? Your desires? Does your "yes" have fruit that follows? We see many people who profess Christ, yet their lives don't follow their words. A person's *words* don't always reflect his or her heart, but a person's *actions* are more indicative of what is in his or her heart. What are your actions saying?

Parable of the Sower

Another parable that can help us determine where we are in our walk with Christ is the Parable of the Sower. It can show us whether we are on fire or lukewarm. For anyone who is a "plant parent," this parable may even hit you a little differently compared to others. But even if you are not, there is such great imagery that you can clearly see how this applies to your own heart and relationship with Jesus.

If you have read through the Gospels, you have noticed that Jesus often used parables to speak to those who were around and willing to listen. Jesus's parables had distinct purposes, particularly revealing truth to those who were willing to hear and believe. In fact, Jesus knew that when He spoke truthful things, it would sometimes fall on deaf ears. He says in Matthew 13:15 that people's hearts had grown calloused, their ears were hard of hearing, and they had shut their eyes.

Essentially, Jesus was saying, "I'm going to say these truths, and I know that some won't care to understand." We have the same issue in our world now with people not wanting to see or hear the truth.

As we read the Parable of the Sower, I hope you can honestly assess, with an open heart, where you currently are in your walk with Christ.

> Listen then to what the parable of the sower means: When anyone hears the message about the kingdom and does not understand it, the evil one comes and snatches away what was sown in their heart. This is the seed sown along the path. The seed falling on rocky ground refers to someone who hears the word and at once receives it with joy. But since they have no root, they last only a short time. When trouble or persecution comes because of the word, they quickly fall away. The seed falling among the thorns refers to someone who hears the word, but the worries of this life and the deceitfulness of wealth choke the word, making it unfruitful. But the seed falling on good soil refers to someone who hears the word and understands it. This is the one who produces a crop, yielding a hundred, sixty or thirty times what was sown" (Matthew 13:18–23, NIV).

I truly do love this parable. It is simple enough so each and every one of us can understand and maybe even be challenged. Jesus gives us four different types of ground or soil that a sower drops seeds on. He drops his seeds in these four places, and each place has a very different reaction to how it grows or doesn't grow. It symbolizes how the Word of God is dropped on our hearts, how we receive it, and if we receive it.

First, we see the ground along the path. No matter if you're a plant parent or not, we all know that if seeds fall onto a path, most likely they won't grow anything worthwhile. Birds (the evil one) snatch those seeds away before anything can happen with them. What could that look like in our lives? The Word of Jesus doesn't rule over anyone's heart who does not believe that Jesus is *Savior* and *Lord* of their lives. This person may hear the Gospel here and there but has no intention of having a God over their lives that is not themselves.

Next is the seed that drops on the rocky soil, which has just a little more hope than the seed on the path. This seed actually has a little sprout that comes from the ground. We can see a little bloom of [insert your favorite plant or flower here], but because the soil probably wasn't the best, and it was surrounded by rocks, the plant sprang up quickly but was scorched by the sun. I imagine this person is one who actually enjoys the message of Jesus but maybe does not have someone discipling them or is not connected with a Christian community. Verse 21 says because this person has no root, his joy is short-lived, and he stumbles away. Most of us have gone to church and felt convicted or encouraged by a message, but then we leave and nothing really changes. While you were joyful on Sunday, there's no root to sustain that joy; while you were determined to change, there's no root to motivate you long term. True sustaining joy and change come from the Holy Spirit, not the willpower to do better after a sermon.

Finally, we have the seed sown among thorns, which does not sound too promising. Verse 22 says this person hears the Word, but the worries of this age and seduction of wealth choke it out, making it unfruitful. I imagine this person is one who loves to hear the encouraging message of Jesus but not the message that challenges us to live differently. I visualize a person who is receiving their daily Word through their Instagram feed instead of their own Bible and local community. They are so used to hearing the uplifting messages of Jesus, and they are shocked when they realize that the life the Bible actually describes for believers is not the Jesus or the life that they signed up for. Jesus tells us that if anyone wants to follow Him, they must deny themselves and daily pick up their cross (Matthew 16:24), but this person may struggle with that because the world says to "live for yourself" and "be true to you."

These three specific soils not only represent those who straight up reject God but also those who claim to be His. The soil represents people's hearts, and all three of these heart types are unfruitful. Matthew 7 confirms that not all who claim to be His are truly His. In verses 21–23 (csb), Jesus says,

> Not everyone who says to Me, 'Lord, Lord!' will enter the kingdom of heaven, but only the one who does the will of My Father in heaven. On that day many will say to me, 'Lord, Lord, didn't we prophesy in Your name, drive out demons in Your name, and do many miracles in Your name?' Then I will announce to them, 'I never knew you! Depart from Me, you lawbreakers!'

These are people who clearly did a lot "in the name of Jesus," but Jesus never really knew them ... and they didn't really know Him either. How can we ensure that we are not one of these people who Jesus never knew? If we say we are followers of Jesus, how do we know that the Word isn't just landing on the path, rocky ground, or thorns? Jesus says we must be born again, and we must continue to walk with Him (John 3:1–7; John 15:1–8).

Nicodemus

If you are not familiar with Nicodemus, he was a Pharisee. As a member of this ancient Jewish sect, he held strict observance of the traditional and written law and devoted himself to superior sanctity. Basically, he was someone who was expected to adhere to the law in almost perfection and looked down on people who could not. Pharisees were often hypocritical or self-righteous. Unlike me, Nicodemus could probably recite the whole Old Testament without a problem. He knew everything about the coming Messiah, but knowing all about someone is a lot different than having a genuine relationship with them.

John 3 describes how Nicodemus privately met with Jesus at night. Remember, Pharisees didn't usually approach Jesus unless they were trying to find fault with Him or publicly humiliate Him. But Nicodemus wanted to have a conversation with Him. Nicodemus likely visited Jesus at night so he wouldn't get caught talking with Him. Nicodemus would have probably been ridiculed by religious leaders if he had been caught in public conversing with the man who dined with sinners and rebuked religious people.

But how often do we act just like Nicodemus? We can be extremely quiet and private about our faith because we would rather not deal with the ridicule or the questions about Jesus or the lifestyle that we live. We say that our faith is private, so there is no need to be open about it; but if our faith is important to us, shouldn't we be eager to talk about it? Jesus is controversial and offensive, and God's Word cuts to the core of each and every one of us, so instead of letting everyone see our potentially offensive faith, we seek Jesus in secret like Nicodemus. Can you relate?

Nicodemus told Jesus that God must be with Him because of the miracles and signs that He had done. Jesus responded, "I assure you: Unless someone is born again, he cannot see the kingdom of God (John 3:3, HCSB). Basically, it isn't your works for Jesus and knowledge about Jesus that saves. Going to church every Sunday, posting Scripture or your favorite celebrity preacher every day on Instagram, or even being a part of a small group will not save you (of course, none of these things are bad in and of themselves). Being born again is the only way to truly know and experience God. As believers, we can't rely on the flesh to give us spiritual results.

Jesus told Nicodemus to **believe** in Him—not to just know a bunch of facts about Him—but to be in a relationship with Him. The fruit of your belief (II Peter 1:5–9) is evidence that you are living in the Spirit rather than in the flesh. You will not do things because it seems like the "Christian thing" to do but because of the loving relationship you have with your Savior. The Pharisees show us that we can look the part and still not truly be in relationship with the one we claim to love.

After Jesus was crucified, Nicodemus was one of the men who buried His body (John 19:39). He brought seventy-five pounds of myrrh and aloes and wrapped Jesus in the tomb. Nicodemus, who was ashamed to be seen speaking to Jesus before, was no longer ashamed. Likewise, when we are reborn, we no longer care who is watching or what they think of us. We simply abide closely to our Lord and allow the Spirit of the living God to transform every area of our lives.

CHAPTER 5:

ABIDE

How do we abide in Jesus? I always love to define words so we are all on the same page. To abide is to "accept or act in accordance with a decision;" "to hold to;" "to remain faithful to." Jesus told His disciples:

> Abide in me, and I in you. As the branch cannot bear fruit by itself, unless it abides in the vine, neither can you, unless you abide in me. I am the vine; you are the branches. Whoever abides in me and I in him, he it is that bears much fruit, for apart from me you can do nothing.
> John 15:4–5 (ESV)

How do we abide in Jesus? We hold onto Him and remain faithful to Him. We accept His way of life rather than our own. William Blake put it this way: "You become what you behold."[4]

Let's examine these definitions more closely:

Accept or act in accordance with a decision

I am sure you have heard something along the lines of, "I've accepted Jesus into my heart." To accept is not passive agreement, but it changes every aspect of your life. Accepting Jesus means we are in an active relationship that is continually growing in service to the Lord. There are boundaries and standards that we live within according to the decision that we made.

Remain faithful to

To abide in Jesus means that we remain faithful to His Word, not our feelings. And as a result, we bear much fruit for His glory. Abiding in Jesus is not something we do once and never have to do it again; instead, it is a daily choice that we must consciously make. In Matthew 16:24 (ESV), Jesus tells His disciples, "If anyone would come after me, let him deny himself and take up his cross and follow me." Just as picking up our cross is a daily act, so it is with abiding. To remain faithful to Jesus, we must truly know Him. It will be a challenge to remain faithful to One whom you do not truly know. Are you reading the Word regularly? Are you in a community of people who will point you to Him? What stirs your affections toward Christ, and what distracts you?

Abiding in Jesus is not something that you will always *feel* like doing. Culture constantly communicates to us that doing what you feel is the only option; however, as believers, we should desire to grow our relationship in the same way we grow any other relationship: get to know the One who saved us. He is worth getting to know!

There will be times when getting in the Word feels more like chore, but I want to encourage you to remain faithful to the One who has proven Himself faithful to you. There are idols at every turn that want to take His place, but remember that they are just broken cisterns that cannot hold water (Jeremiah 2:13). Only Jesus can give you the living water that can truly satisfy you (John 4:10).

Pruning and Bearing Fruit

Abiding in Jesus will look different for each of us because our stories are immensely different. Nonetheless, there will be truth that applies to every one of us. For example, God will prune things out of our lives so that we can bear fruit for Him. The pruning seasons generally aren't the easiest or most comforting times in our lives. The purpose of pruning is to reduce the influence or growth of something by removing unwanted parts. Pruning especially increases fruitfulness and growth.

Paul tells us in Galatians that the flesh desires what is against the Spirit, and the Spirit desires what is against the flesh (Galatians 5:16–17). Paul even admitted to struggling with this himself in Romans 7:18–23 where he talks about doing the very things he knew that he should not be doing, but he still struggled to stop.

When God prunes our lives, He removes the desires of the flesh and "works in [us], both to will and to work for his good pleasure" (Philippians 2:13, ESV). This is not always a simple process, and that's where abiding comes in. Abiding in Jesus means embracing the pruning seasons of our lives (which never stop) so that we please and serve the One who saved us.

As believers, we are justified by God but sanctified daily until we meet Him face to face. First Thessalonians 5:23 says, "Now may the God of peace himself sanctify you completely, and may your whole spirit and soul and body be kept blameless at the coming of our Lord Jesus Christ." If you are living your life as a follower of Jesus, but you are still gratifying the desires of the flesh without conviction, maybe you should ask yourself: "Am I truly abiding in Jesus?"

To be clear, I'm not saying after you give your life to Jesus you will no longer struggle with sin, but there is a difference between occasionally stumbling versus living unrepentantly without conviction in those sins. Galatians 5:19–21 lists the obvious works of the flesh: sexual immorality, jealousy, and drunkenness to name a few. As I said before, alcohol was a sin for me that I was not willing or ready to give up. After professing my love for Jesus, my desire for alcohol did not just vanish. God's pruning was not expeditious; it took time before I realized that He was truly better than what I was trying to find while being drunk. To abide in Jesus, we must embrace the pruning seasons in our lives and trust that He not only saves us and keeps us but He also empowers us by His Spirit to "keep in step with the Spirit" and produce the Fruit of the Spirit (Galatians 5:22–25).

God may start to nudge you to end certain relationships that hold you back from Him. Or, maybe He will begin stirring your heart to forgive a certain friend. If God continues to push you away from the things that do not line up with His desires or commandments, and you are constantly resisting, it may be a good time to ask, "Am I truly abiding in Jesus?"

Delight

As believers, we shouldn't grudgingly abide in Jesus but rather delight in Him as we abide. I believe marriage is a perfect example. If people saw me loathing every moment of my marriage with my husband, they would wonder if I truly loved him. If my life does not reflect the love and sacrifice that a covenantal marriage is supposed to have, it is only right that you wonder what is really going on.

It is the same with our relationship with the Lord. If we obey His commands, yet despise every minute of it, people will wonder if we really love God. They may doubt how good God actually is.

Psalm 119 is a great chapter to dig into because it talks about delighting in God. It is the longest chapter in the Bible and is packed with verses about delighting in God's Word. If you are delighting in the Word of God, then you will also delight in Him. This chapter is packed with prayers to the Lord that I enjoy praying daily. John 15:7 tells us that if we abide in Jesus and His words abide in us, then we can ask whatever we want, and it will be done. How differently would our lives look if we prayed these words with a soft and authentic heart to Jesus every day?

> Teach me, O Lord, the way of your statutes;
>> and I will keep it to the end.
> Give me understanding, that I may keep your law
>> and observe it with my whole heart.
> Lead me in the path of your commandments,
>> for I delight in it.
> Incline my heart to your testimonies,
>> and not to selfish gain!
> Turn my eyes from looking at worthless things;
>> and give me life in your ways.
> Confirm to your servant your promise,
>> that you may be feared.
> Turn away the reproach that I dread,
>> for your rules are good.
> Behold, I long for your precepts;
>> in your righteousness give me life!
> Psalm 119:33–40 (ESV)

CHAPTER 6:

THE LIFE OF PAUL

If you could hang out with any biblical figure besides Jesus, who would it be?

Well, my answer has always been Paul. His story is one that never ceases to amaze me. If you do not know anything about Paul, he was famous for murdering Christians. He was a Pharisee who despised what Christians were saying about Jesus and had men, women, and children thrown into prison or killed for their beliefs. Incredibly, Paul is the guy who wrote most of the New Testament. He could probably recite the Torah (Old Testament) to you. He, like Nicodemus, probably knew everything *about* the coming Messiah, but he did not have a genuine relationship *with* Him.

There is a huge difference between head knowledge and heart knowledge. Even if you could recite the entire book of Leviticus to me (good luck), it does not mean a thing if you do not have a genuine relationship with the One you know so much about.

43

There is obviously a ton that we can learn from Paul, but I love looking at the transformation of his life from when he was Saul, the Christian persecutor, to when he became Paul, an apostle of Christ.

Does your life resemble Paul's at all? Maybe you have not experienced a blinding light from heaven and Jesus's audible voice, but what about the unmistakable life change? Paul didn't say one thing with his words and another with his actions. After his encounter with Christ, his whole life changed. Because he lived the life he proclaimed, he faced plenty of hardships up until his death.

Saul: The Christian Murderer

I've already touched on the fact that before his encounter with the Lord, Paul persecuted the Church. He ordered men, women, and children to be thrown into prison or killed if they attempted to spread the good news of Jesus. I do not think anyone reading this has probably persecuted the church in this way (and if you have, clearly God can still use you), but maybe you have always thrown a little shade at the Church. Maybe you've debated any chance you could about how anyone who follows Jesus is brainwashed. Perhaps you have called Christians lazy people who just need a prop to make them feel better about life. Or, maybe you just never really cared—you never cared to prove to people that what they believed was wrong.

No matter where you fall on the spectrum, you were living a life that opposed Jesus. You were living a life separated from God and dead in your trespasses and sins, following the course of the world, and carrying out the passions of the flesh (Ephesians 2:1–3, paraphrased). Paul didn't even realize his actions opposed God at first, but when God showed him the error of his ways, he repented. When

God removed the scales from his eyes (Acts 9:18), he recognized how sinful he was.

What about you? Before you were a believer, what sins were evident in your life? Mine? Sexual immorality, drunkenness, pride, and putting my hope in my own works instead of the finished work of the cross and Jesus—just to name a few.

When you look at your own life, are you still living in the same sins as you did before you knew Jesus? Did you accept Christ into your life and continue to live in the darkness and ways of the world? Remember, there is a difference between stumbling versus living a consistent lifestyle gratifying the flesh. If Paul's lifestyle *after* he dedicated his life to Christ looked no different from his lifestyle *before*, then everyone around him would have noticed the disconnect. They would have seen that although he was saying that he believed, clearly he did not.

Likewise, there is no way we can encounter Jesus and live the same way we did before. Be honest with yourself and ask, "Has my life changed from before Christ to after?"

Saul's Encounter with Jesus

Paul's encounter with Jesus changed everything. He went from killing and despising the name of Jesus to boldly proclaiming His name everywhere he went. The transformation was dramatic and undeniable. As Paul was on the road to Damascus, his plans to continue in his lifestyle were drastically changed.

As he traveled and was nearing Damascus, a light from heaven suddenly flashed around him. Falling to the ground he heard a voice saying to him, "Saul, Saul, why are you persecuting me?" "Who are You, Lord?" Saul said.

"I am Jesus, the One you are persecuting," he replied. "But get up and go into the city, and you will be told what you must do."

Acts 9:3–7 (CSB)

The bright light literally blinded Saul. Three days after losing his vision, a disciple of Jesus named Ananias was sent to heal Saul and give him a message. When Ananias laid his hands on Saul, he received his sight, was filled with the Holy Spirit, and then was baptized. Paul was quickly humbled and realized His need for Jesus. And he responded when the Lord got his attention.

While many of us today will probably not have an experience like Saul's, God still reaches out to get our attention. In what ways has God done this in your life? When I truly encountered Jesus, it was not during the times that I went to church so I could look good or when I posted my favorite verses on Snapchat or Instagram for everyone to see—it was the moment I realized my desperate need for Jesus. I realized that when I come face to face with a holy and righteous God, all the moments that I thought were important did not really matter at all.

"Katrina, what would you say if you died and God asked, 'Why should I let you in?'" was the question that God used to convict me of all my sin and reveal my real need for Him. I realized that all my "good works" would not be "good enough" to allow me to enter into the presence of God. My "righteousness" was not the answer at all—the cross was.

So, I will ask again, what did this moment look like for you? We all have different stories. Our testimonies won't be the same, and our lives will look different from one another's ... but we should all have a common story where Jesus intervenes in our lives, amid all our mess, and we recognize our neediness—our need for the love and grace of God to come in and radically transform our lives.

Have you identified that moment when God convicted you of all your sin and changed your life? If it is not "godly grief" that led you to repentance (I Corinthians 7:10, csb), then that isn't the moment I am referring to. If you are struggling to think of that moment when God convicted you, and life-change followed, I challenge you to wrestle with the thought of encountering Jesus and invite Him to transform you completely like He did Saul.

Paul: Apostle of Jesus Christ

Up to this point, we have seen Saul's life before Christ and his encounter with Christ. Now let's discuss how Saul became Paul, and how he initially responded to the good news of Jesus.

> So Ananias left and entered the house. Then he placed his hands on him and said, "Brother Saul, the Lord Jesus who appeared to you on the road you were traveling, has sent me so that you can regain your sight and be filled with the Holy Spirit." At once something like scales fell from his eyes, and he regained his sight. Then he got up and was baptized....
> Saul was with the disciples in Damascus for some days. Immediately he began proclaiming Jesus in the synagogues: "He is the Son of God."
> Acts 9:17–20 (hcsb)

Immediately after Paul realized Jesus was and is who He claimed to be, Paul immediately got baptized. Baptism subsequently comes right after belief, especially in the book of Acts. Oftentimes, one will call themselves a believer and never get baptized after their belief. Is this a requirement for salvation? Absolutely not. It is by grace alone, through faith alone that we are saved (Ephesians 2:8). But we cannot ignore all the times in the New Testament when someone believed and was baptized right away.

For example, think of Philip and the Ethiopian in Acts 8. God told Philip to go and speak with an Ethiopian man who was reading Scripture on his way home. The Ethiopian did not understand what he was reading, so Philip explained and guided him in understanding it (Acts 8:30–31). After Philip explained the good news about Jesus by using the Scripture they were reading, the man said, "Look, there's water! What would keep me from being baptized?" (Acts 8:36, HCSB).

As soon as this Ethiopian man received understanding and believed with his heart, he did not delay his proclamation of what he believed. So, what is water baptism, and why is it so important? Baptism by immersion symbolizes new life in the believer. It symbolizes union with Christ in His death, burial, and resurrection both spiritually and physically.

Maybe you're thinking, "Eh ... that's nice, but it just doesn't sound that important." Honestly, I thought the same thing. I didn't get baptized until two years after I became a believer. I was not intentionally trying to hide my love and declaration for Jesus, but I truly didn't realize what I was telling the world with the act of baptism. For example, after I got married, I did not have to wear a wedding band for the marriage to be official. The band shows the world that I clearly belong to someone. Baptism, in the same way, doesn't solid-ify our eternity but announces our love for Jesus and Jesus alone. It shows and tells the world that we are surrendering all to Jesus. Paul says it this way in Galatians 2:19–20 (CSB):

> For through the law I have died to the law, so that I might live for God. I have been crucified with Christ and I no longer live, but Christ lives in me. The life I now live in the body, I live by faith in the Son of God, who loved me and gave Himself for me.

Paul's Community

After Paul's conversion, he spent time with the disciples in Damascus for some days. I am not sure exactly how many days "some days" were specifically, but he spent about three years in Damascus before fleeing due to persecution. We can assume he became familiar with basic Christianity as he spent time with the other disciples. Paul's interaction with fellow believers did not end when he left Damascus; he continued to surround himself with believers regularly.

I often hear professing believers say, "My relationship with God is between me and God" as an excuse not to be in community with other believers. Having other believers around is always vital, but in my opinion, it's especially important when you first become a fol-lower of Christ. For example, Paul was probably not only learning a plethora of new ideas but also unlearning some of the things he had believed to be true but were actually lies.

Pharisees often looked down on people who sinned. Although Pharisees need grace just as much as others, their self-righteous-ness oftentimes would not allow them to see the plank in their own eye (Matthew 7:1–5). What about you? If you grew up in the Bible Belt or in a Christian household, maybe there were things you also had to unlearn during your transformation. Maybe you believed that since Jesus already died on the cross for our sins, you could live however you wanted? Perhaps you believed you weren't truly saved unless you could speak in tongues. The list could also go on and on. Thankfully, God never intended for us to "figure it all out" on our own—He gave us a body of believers to help us. Are you surrounding yourself with others who can help you understand the faith, rebuke you when needed, and walk alongside you? Community is a gift from God that we must not take for granted.

Paul Took Action Immediately

Lastly, we see that Paul immediately started to proclaim the good news. He went from synagogue to synagogue proclaiming who Jesus was to anyone who would listen. He went to places where he knew people would not agree with him (hence why he left Damascus and many other places to flee persecution) and consistently shared the good news.

He did not change the message of the gospel to appease those around him; instead, he walked by the Spirit, realizing that each person desperately needed Christ. If you believe that every single person will either spend eternity in heaven or in hell, you understand why he felt such an urgency to share despite the incredible persecution.

We can't assume that our lives alone are enough for people to see Jesus in us. Of course, we want to reflect Christ, but we have to proclaim Him as well. Romans 10:14 (NLT) says,

But how can they call on him to save them unless they believe in him? And how can they believe in him if they have never heard about him? And how can they hear about him unless someone tells them?

Telling the good news of Jesus is not reserved only for pastors from a pulpit but for all who call Jesus their Lord and Savior.

Sharing Your Faith

As a lover of apologetics (the ability to defend what you believe), I've grown a lot in this area, and I continue to grow. The thought of telling someone what they should believe can be scary for many reasons.

What if they ask you a question that you can't answer?

What if they truly do not agree with your beliefs at all?

What if they have been hurt by someone who claimed to be a believer?

It is so much easier to just be nice and hope they ask you the perfect question that you can confidently answer. While there are many reasons why boldly sharing your beliefs is scary, I think we usually overcomplicate it. Trust me, I know I do. Personally, I sometimes forget that the Holy Spirit is dwelling inside me and that I do not have to do this in my own strength.

Are you aware of the Holy Spirit and His work in your life? Maybe you have heard about the idea of the Spirit, but you only know Christianity in the way that I knew it: work as hard as you can to be a good person. Or maybe, depending on your background, you have heard of the Holy Spirit as something you "catch" sometimes, not as the Spirit of the living God dwelling inside you. Either way, the Holy Spirit, who is our helper and friend, is here to guide us in this world and to help us live a life pleasing to God. We have to remember that He is with us and won't abandon us when we have conversations with others about the good news of Jesus.

How often do you take inventory regarding your walk with Jesus? Have you truly encountered Him and been wrecked by His love and grace? Jesus's love and grace should invigorate you to show the world Whose you are in the act of baptism, to be in a community that draws you closer to Jesus and away from the world, and to proclaim the good news to everyone.

Questioning Saul's Transformation

Paul's life-change was evident to everyone; it was even unbelievable to some at first. When people heard that Paul was now a follower of Jesus, they most likely remembered his past. When Jesus told Ananias to find Paul and lay hands on him, Ananias was a little skeptical about the task. His response was, "Lord, I have heard from many people about this man, how much harm he has done to Your saints..." (Acts 9:13, LEB). And a few verses later when Paul was proclaiming Christ, people said, "Isn't this the man who, in Jerusalem, was destroying those who called on this name?" (Acts 9:21, HCSB).

Like Paul, people may be a little doubtful when they see our transformation. They may wonder, "Isn't she (or he) the one who used to _____?" You can fill in the blank with any of the sins that God tore you away from.

52

"Isn't she the one who used to gossip behind everyone's back?"

"Isn't he the one that used to sleep around with everyone?"

"Isn't she the one who was always deceitful?"

The list is endless. Your list likely won't include "Isn't she (he) the one that killed Christians?" but people still may genuinely not believe there has been a change in you. However, there is no way people would believe that Christ saved Paul from himself and his sin if he still walked around killing Christians. I'm sure Paul heard what others were saying about him, but I'm also sure that Paul was so enthralled in his new relationship with Jesus that it didn't matter what they were saying about his past. Paul's consistency in word **and** deed eventually showed everyone that his life truly was different.

I pray that you, like Paul, are so captivated with Jesus that when people bring up your past, it doesn't even phase you. You now understand that you were dead in your sins and in need of a Savior—that not only your present and future sins are forgiven, but so are those past sins as well. While people may truly wonder if your life has changed, it should be evident that Jesus has entered your life and dwells within you. In word and deed, people can see that your life truly is different from the life you once lived—not because of anything specific that you did but because of Jesus invading every area of your life.

> Don't you know that the unrighteous will not inherit God's kingdom? Do not be deceived: No sexually immoral people, idolaters, adulterers, or anyone practicing homosexuality, no thieves, greedy people, drunkards, verbally abusive

people, or swindlers will inherit God's kingdom. *And some of you used to be like this. But you were washed, you were sanctified, you were justified in the name of the Lord Jesus and by the Spirit of our God.*

I Corinthians 6:9–11 (HCSB, emphasis added)

CHAPTER 7:

LOVE VS. TOLERATE

In my own experience, one of the hardest transitions after giving your life to Jesus is realizing those who are closest to you may not have the same love for Him as you do. After giving our lives to Christ, we are often on a spiritual high and can talk about Jesus all day long. We talk about Jesus and what He has done for us personally and what He can do for everyone who is willing to listen. Jesus, now being most important person in your life, may not be the most important person in others' lives.

How do you interact with those who want nothing to do with Whom you love most?

The simple answer: **we love them anyway.** But, what does it look like to truly love someone who disagrees with you? We live in a culture that tosses the word "love" around loosely. Not only do we loosely use the word, but we also use the word "tolerate" in its place. To tolerate someone or something means to allow the existence, occurrence, or practice of without interference (something that one does not necessarily like or agree with).[5]

Maybe you read that definition and thought to yourself, "That sounds like love to me." People may wonder why we would interfere with anyone we disagree with. It isn't any of our business if someone wants to live their life a certain way. However, we would never say that if we knew someone was in danger because of the choices they were making.

Share With Urgency

Picture this scenario: You have a friend who just bought a new house, and she never wants to leave it. You think it's a little strange that she only leaves the house to check the mail or walk the dog, but she isn't hurting anyone, so what's the big deal? But then one day, you pull up to her house and it is on fire—but instead of busting down the door and dragging her out, you say, "Well, I really do not want to bother her. I know how much she loves her new house, so I won't intrude." Sounds insane, right? You know that wouldn't happen. You would call 9-1-1 and bust through the doors to try and save her.

It is just as insane to be a follower of Jesus, believe His words in John 14:6 (CSB) ("I am the way, the truth, and the life. No one comes to the Father except through me."), and go about your day or life without saying anything about it. We are talking about eternity here. If our friends and loved ones' physical lives are important, how much more important are their souls? Matthew 10:28 (ESV) says it this way: "And do not fear those who kill the body but cannot kill the soul. Rather fear him who can destroy both soul and body in hell."

Let me be clear. I'm not saying that every conversation you have with people must be about Jesus. I'm not saying that you have to stand on the street corner yelling, "Turn or burn!" But what I am saying is you can't claim you truly care about others and care more about their short lives here on earth than their eternity.

I have seen believers completely withdraw from any family or friends who do not know Jesus. They do not want to get caught in the messi-ness of tolerating their sin, but they also do not want to say anything about it either. So, they just remove themselves completely. I'm not calling you out—I am talking about myself. I professed my new love for Jesus and hoped that anyone who didn't have a relationship with Jesus would just see a difference in my life and ask me about it. I did not want to have to tell anyone that the life they were living was a life that was in opposition of the One who gave it to them. So, I'll ask again: What does it truly mean to love someone who does not agree with you? Paul gives us great advice in I Corinthians on how to engage with those who do not believe.

> For though I am free from all, I have made myself a servant
> to all, that I might win more of them. To the Jews I became
> as a Jew, in order to win Jews. To those under the law I
> became as one under the law (though not being under the
> law myself) that I might win those under the law. To those
> outside the law I became as one outside the law (not being
> outside the law of God but under the law of Christ) that I
> might win those outside the law. To the weak I became weak,
> that I might win the weak. I have become all things to all
> people, that by all means I might save some. I do it all for the
> sake of the gospel, that I may share with them in its blessing.
> 1 Corinthians 9:19–23 (ESV)

In verse 22, Paul says "become all things to all people." That is our answer. Paul is not saying to indulge in sinful acts to win those who do not know Jesus. That would result in a confusing message to others because you would be contradicting what you say you believe.

Paul says in Galatians that we are called to be free, but not to use our freedom as an opportunity for the flesh, but to serve others in love (Galatians 5:13, paraphrase). Paul is saying that while pleasing God first, he made sure that his life was not a hindrance to the gospel. For example, if you have ever read Galatians, it is all about Paul communicating to the Gentiles that it is by faith alone and grace alone that we are free. (Some were starting to believe that you had to be circumcised to be right with God, which ultimately meant that Jesus's death on the cross was not enough to save.) Although Paul knew that one was saved by faith and grace, he also circumcised Timothy in Acts 16. Why? Timothy's mother was a Jewish woman. Paul demonstrated his freedom in Christ among the Jews to augment the gospel witness in the Jewish areas. Paul was not doing this out of fear but out of love. To some, that might sound like a contradiction, but he was living out the Corinthian verse above, becoming all things to all people to win them for Christ.

Becoming All Things to All People

Here's a modern-day example that you can relate to. Picture this scenario: I get invited by some vegan friends (who don't personally know Jesus as their Lord and Savior) to come over for dinner next week. Of course, I'll go. If you know me at all, I am not a vegan. Unless the Lord comes down and blinds me like He did Paul on the way to Damascus, I don't plan on becoming vegan either (no offense), but I do love good friends and food!

My vegan friends ask me if I can bring an appetizer for the night, and they will make a few entrees and side dishes. Although I have never had a cauliflower wing in my life, I would probably make them for the group that night. Why? Not because they suddenly sound delicious but because I want them to know that I can sacrifice my desire for real chicken and enjoy the things that they enjoy. I want them to know that it is not a problem to sacrifice for them because that is what love does. I don't want the gospel to be hindered because I decide to throw some chicken wings in my vegan friends' faces. Paul might have put it like this: *To those who are vegan, I become vegan, so that I might win the vegans for Christ.*

That may be a silly example but fill in the blanks. To those who are _____, are you becoming like them in the hope that their souls are saved? Remember, you're not becoming "like them" as far as sinning with them, but "like them" so you can share the gospel with them, sacrificing and loving them the way that they need to be loved so they will be open to hearing about Jesus.

CHAPTER 8:

ASSURANCE

Eternity. What do you believe about it? I know that we all have heard the word eternity before, but let's make sure we are on the same page. The definition of eternity is *infinite* or *unending* time. Ultimately, what you believe about eternity will directly affect how you live your life.

Eternity was something I never really thought of until the conversation that God used to convict me of my sinfulness. Eternity was something that I didn't plan on thinking about until I was a lot older and closer to death. But we have no idea when our eyes will permanently shut, and we meet God face to face. So, if you haven't really thought about eternity much, I hope God uses the message in this book to do so.

Jesus tells us that there are only two possible routes when it comes to eternity. First, there is a broad road that leads to destruction or death (Matthew 7:13). Not only is this road broad, but Jesus also says there are *many* who go through it. Yikes. And many of those people will believe that they are on the right path, but they are not (Matthew 7:22).

The second route that Jesus talks about is the narrow road that leads to life (Matthew 7:14). Those are the only two options. This may be a silly example, but hear me out. I love rollercoasters. The best and worst part about rollercoasters though, in my opinion, is how fast they are. You wait in line forever (if you don't have a fast pass), you buckle yourself in for the ride, and then the ride is over in twenty seconds or less. That's the first thing that comes to my mind when I think about this life in comparison to eternity. It may feel like we are here for a long time, but in comparison to eternity, this life is the twenty-second rollercoaster ride that you waited hours to experience. James says it this way: "Yet you do not know what tomorrow will bring. What is your life? For you are a mist that appears for a little time and then vanishes" (James 4:14, ESV).

How do we have assurance that we are on the narrow road, not the wide, destructive road? Spiritual deception is a real and dangerous thing, and Peter tells us that our adversary, the devil, is prowling around like a roaring lion looking for anyone—but especially believers—to devour (I Peter 5:8). I continue to reference Matthew 7:22 because the people who heard those words from Jesus fell into the trap of spiritual deception. They thought they had assurance and that they would be greeted with, "Well done, good and faithful servant" (Mattew 25:21, CSB), but instead they heard, "I never knew you. Depart from me," (Matthew 7:23, CSB).

Examine Yourself Regularly

I hope this does not sound like you should walk around being fearful of death; remember, Jesus defeated death. But I hope you are now wondering, "How can I be sure I'm right with the Lord?" Second Corinthians 13:5 (csb) is a great starting point:

> Test yourselves to see if you are in the faith. Examine yourselves. Or do you yourselves not recognize that Jesus Christ is in you?—unless you fail the test.

Test yourself. Examine yourself. In the notes of my study Bible it says,

> These present-tense verbs [**test, examine**] could be translated "keep on testing" and "keep on examining". A believer never gets beyond the need for regular self-examination.[6]

What does that look like practically in the life of the believer? Before I dive into my thoughts, I want you to take a minute and ask the Lord for a soft heart while you read these ideas. Ask Him to reveal any pride that may be hidden in your heart. Maybe you don't have closed fists and intentional pride, but unintentional pride may result in the same behavior. You may be able to fool a lot of people, or even yourself at times, but God is not the One to try to mislead.

Okay ... here we go. Above all else, have you repented and believed? Maybe you read that, and you think, "Next—of course, I have!" Slow down. Remember Matthew 7:22? Have you repented and believed? Have you turned from your sin and submitted to Jesus in every area of your life? Have you made the decision that Jesus is not only the Savior of your life but Lord as well? Often, we do not mind Jesus saving us from hell, but we do not want Him to have a say in our mundane, day-to-day life. Is Jesus Lord **and** Savior of your life?

I mentioned before that I called myself a follower of Jesus while giving Him only certain parts of my life that I was comfortable with Him having. I thought, *Sure, I'll remain celibate until I find my husband, but I will still get drunk on the weekends.* I wanted Jesus to save me, but I did not want Jesus to tell me how to live my life.

Is Jesus Lord **and** Savior of your life?

Digging Into the Word for Assurance

First John is a great book to study for anyone struggling with assurance of salvation. In this book, John maps out three essential components of saving knowledge of God:

1. faith in Jesus Christ,
2. obedient response to God's commands,
3. and love for God and others from the heart.

We have assurance of salvation based on the work of Jesus on the cross and His resurrection; therefore, our continual belief in the cross should have a direct effect on our life. The churchy word for that effect in our life is "sanctification." Sanctification is the action of making something or someone holy. It is the *ongoing process* of our lives being transformed by the Spirit and the continual change of our heart and mind (Romans 12:2). That continual change will impact our love for others and, most importantly, for God.

First John 1:6 is a verse that directly addresses the hypocrisy of people saying they are following Jesus while living a life that denies Him: "If we say, 'We have fellowship with him,' and yet we walk in darkness, we are lying and are not practicing the truth."

Not to be repetitive, but I think it is worth asking and thinking about this again: Have you repented and believed? Is Jesus Lord <u>and</u> Savior of your life? Are you saying He is Lord while you walk in a way that opposes His Word? If so, you are lying and not practicing the truth—not my words, but John's.

If you realize this is you, there is grace for that. "He is faithful and righteous to forgive us our sins and cleanse us from all unrighteousness" (I John 1:9, CSB). Turn away from the darkness, let go of the sin that so easily entangles you (Hebrews 12:1–3), and turn to Jesus.

If there are times where you think the Bible is confusing (and there are some), this is not one of them. Instead of my trying to explain what John is saying, read his words for yourself:

> My little children, I am writing you these things so that you may not sin. But if anyone does sin, we have an advocate with the Father—Jesus Christ the Righteous One. He Himself is the propitiation [atonement] for our sins, and not only for ours, but also for those of the whole world. This is how we are sure that we have come to know Him: by keeping His commands. The one who says, "I have come to know Him," yet doesn't keep His commands, is a liar, and the truth is not in him. But whoever keeps His word, truly in him the love of God is perfected. This is how we know we are in Him: The one who says he remains in Him should walk just as He walked.
>
> Dear friends, I am not writing you a new command but an old command that you have had from the beginning. The old command is the message you have heard. Yet I am writing you a new command, which is true in Him and in you,

because the darkness is passing away and the true light is
already shining.

I John 2:1–8 (HCSB)

"This is how we know we are in Him ... ," or in other words, this is
how we have assurance. Are you sure of your salvation? Are you sure
that you have fully accepted Jesus into your life? Have you repented
of walking in darkness? It is easy for us to *say* we are following Jesus
with all our heart, mind, and strength, yet we look no different than
the world. Do not assume. Be confident in whose you are. Are you
truly His?

CHAPTER 9:

DON'T BE FOOLED

Do not love the world or the things that belong to the world.
If anyone loves the world, love for the Father is not in him.
For everything that belongs to the world—the lust of the flesh,
the lust of the eyes, and the pride in one's lifestyle—is not from
the Father, but is from the world. And the world with its lust is
passing away, but the one who does God's will remains forever.
I John 2:15–17 (HCSB)

If you are not His, the only other option is that you are the world's
and under the spell of the devil. C.S Lewis puts it like this: "Indeed
the safest road to Hell is the gradual one—the gentle slope, soft
underfoot, without sudden turnings, without milestones, without
signposts." What Lewis is saying here is that most of the time, the
devil is crafty enough to convince you that your sin isn't that big of
a deal. Satan will have you under the impression that if your sins
aren't "too big" or "too bad" then you should be fine.

Do you belong to Jesus or do you belong to the world? John says
that that "the lust of the flesh, the lust of the eyes, and the pride in

[your] lifestyle is not from the Father" (I John 2:17, HCSB). Lust and pride can reveal themselves in a plethora of ways in one's lifestyle and will even look different from person to person.

So, what are some different sin patterns in each of these areas? Lust of the flesh? Sexual immorality or drunkenness. Lust of the eyes? Lusting, coveting, or jealousy. Pride in your lifestyle? Well, obviously... thinking you are better than everyone else. (Pro tip: don't compare yourself to other sinners. You will either look better than you are or feel like you will never measure up).

Although these examples are appropriate and accurate, there is a deeper issue at the root: it's not just about what we do with the material objects of this world; the problem is that they diminish our love for the Father. When we consistently and unrepentantly dethrone Jesus and replace Him with anything else, there should be a genuine concern if love for Jesus is truly there. What we replace Jesus with is an idol, and that idol will never truly satisfy.

Enthroning Idols Instead of Jesus

What are some idols that you put on the throne instead of Jesus? Don't just skim pass this part but truly think about it. Are the idols that come to mind—whether it is your significant other or screen time—something you are actively trying to fight against? Or, are you okay with your idols being more worth your time and attention than Jesus is?

In Jeremiah 2:13, God says that His people abandoned Him, the fountain of living water, for broken cisterns that could not hold any water. Jesus also said something very similar in John, saying that whoever drinks the water that He gives, will never thirst again (John

4:13–14). What are these verses conveying? None of those idols that you are trying to make your god will ever be sufficient. It would be silly to continue to try to fill something that has cracks or holes in it. The object that you fill will hold water for a time, but it will never remain full. Likewise, when you put your hope in other things, it's like pouring water into a cracked jar. Your heart needs so much more than the gods you are trying to create can give. They may make you feel good in the moment, but the reason you keep going back is because they are never enough.

Paul was dealing with a similar situation which compelled him to warn the Corinthian believers of Israel's past. After the Lord delivered them from Egypt and provided for them on the way to the Promised Land, the Israelites claimed the name of God but sadly looked no different from the pagans around them. Similarly, the Corinthians thought that they could please the Lord while at the same time partake in the lifestyle of the pagans around them.

First Corinthians 10:21 (csb) says, "You cannot drink the cup of the Lord and the cup of demons. You cannot share in the Lord's table and the table of demons." What the Israelites and Corinthians dealt with is not foreign to our world today. We cannot say that we believe God is all powerful while we burn sage to cleanse the energy. We cannot say that we believe that God is omniscient and sovereign while we manifest our deepest desires. We cannot give thanks to both God and the universe. Romans 12:2 (esv) says,

> Do not be conformed to this world, but be transformed by the renewal of your mind, that by testing you may discern what is the will of God, what is good and acceptable and perfect."

Do not fall for the tricks that the world is constantly trying to pull. The world and everyone in it want you to believe that you can look exactly like the world and still hear, "Well done, good and faithful servant" (Matthew 25:21, CSB) when we meet Jesus at the end. The world wants you to believe that you can pick and choose what truth is and that everyone is the source of their own.

Do not be conformed to the patterns of this world. We must renew our minds, or the world will try and convince us that our flesh isn't "too bad"—that the sexual immorality, drunkenness, pride, and lust are not that big of a deal after all. Please do not be fooled. You are either led by the Spirit, or you are led by the flesh. "Therefore, my dear friends, flee from idolatry" (I Corinthians 10:14, HCSB).

CHAPTER 10:

IT IS FINISHED

What is the gospel? Why is it good news? Are you able to articulate this news to yourself and others? Where I'm at, in the Bible Belt, we do all the church things well, but often we do not fully understand *why* we are doing them. Or, we aren't doing any of those things and still claiming to be His while living a life that looks no different from the world.

As we near the end of the book, I truly hope that you have been challenged and come closer to the Lord, but I do not feel like this book would be complete without making sure you understand what it truly means to be a follower of Jesus. We understand that Jesus died for our sins, but what does that really mean? How does His sacrifice impact everything about us? This will not be a chapter telling you how to be a better Christian; it will simply be an explanation of the gospel and what that means for us sinners who are in need of God's grace.

You probably remember the story of Adam and Eve. They were made in the image of God and had a perfect relationship with each other and God, but then they disobeyed God in Genesis 3. God gave them boundaries to live within, and they decided to do their own thing instead. That choice severed their perfect relationship with the creator and ours; the consequence was death (Genesis 2:16–17).

Since then, every human being has disobeyed God. You, me, and everyone we know have stepped outside of the boundaries that God has given us (more times than we can count), and we deserve death (Romans 6:23).

The Israelites (God's chosen people through whom He revealed Himself to the world) had a way to be forgiven of their sins by sacrificing animals. I know, it's kind of strange with our western mindset, but stay with me. God is holy and perfect, and we have already discussed that we are not even close to holy. A holy, loving, and just God cannot be any of those things if He allows sins to go unpunished. So, instead of the Israelites getting what they deserved (death), the animal took the place of the sinner, and the sinner walked away completely forgiven and right with God.

Soon enough, the Israelites were taking the sacrifices for granted. They were sacrificing the animals but living a life that did not look any different from the heathen nations around them. Isaiah 1:11–15 (HCSB) says,

> "What are all your sacrifices to me?" asks the Lord. "I have
> had enough of burnt offerings and rams and the fat of well-
> fed cattle; I have no desire for the blood of bulls, lambs,
> or male goats. When you come to appear before Me, who
> requires this from you—this trampling of My courts? Stop
> bringing useless offerings. Your incense is detestable to
> Me. New Moons and Sabbaths and the calling of solemn

assemblies—I cannot stand iniquity with a festival. I hate your New Moons and prescribed festivals. They have become a burden to Me; I am tired of putting up with them. When you lift up your hands in prayers, I will refuse to look at you; even if you offer countless prayers, I will not listen. Your hands are covered with blood."

I mean, that is deep (you should read all of Isaiah 1). The continual sacrifices of the Israelites had become meaningless to them and to God.

A Great King

We see throughout the Old Testament that God promised to send a ruler to bring peace and harmony and to defeat what is evil in the world (Genesis 3:15, Isaiah 7:14, Isaiah 9:2–7, Jeremiah 23:5–8). We needed a way to deal with the sin, wickedness, and suffering, and everyone was excited to have a king who would finally do that!

That is where Jesus came in. Jesus, God in the flesh, came down to live a life that we could not live. He lived a life that was completely pleasing to God the Father, then died a horrific death on a cross as an innocent man. People thought they were receiving a king, but then He was killed. How? Why? Because while they were looking for a king, He came as the final sacrificial lamb. The hope that they had in Him, the hope of the wicked defeated, the hope of a new life, was lost at the cross (or, so they thought). The last thing Jesus said on the cross was, "It is finished!" before He gave up His spirit (John 19:30, HCSB). It was a very odd thing to say as He was dying a death He didn't deserve with people ridiculing and mocking Him as it was happening. What exactly was finished?

Romans 6:23 (HCSB) tells us that "the wages of sin is death." What that means for us is that we have earned the death penalty because of our continual sinning against a holy, righteous, and perfect God. But thankfully, the verse does not end there: "The wages of sin is death, but the gift of God is eternal life in Christ Jesus our Lord." So, when Jesus uttered, "It is finished" before giving up His spirit (John 19:30, HCSB), He declared that our debt has been paid in full!

Let me give you an example that is not even comparable to what Jesus did on the cross but hopefully can bring some clarity. If you have gone to college, you are probably aware of student loans. Even if you personally do not have any, you probably know of people who do. According to a 2021 study on education data, the average federal student loan debt is $36,510 per borrower. For private student loans the average is $54,921.[7] I personally know of people who have close to $100,000 of student loan debt that they have to pay off. If you are one of those people who are currently paying off that debt, imagine one day you head to your account to make your monthly payment, and the balance is cleared. The debt is paid in FULL. What kind of joy would that bring you?

We could also look at Barabbas. We don't know a ton about Barabbas, but we do know that he was also on trial (basically death row) at the same time as Jesus. Barabbas was not a good guy. John 18:40 tells us that he was a "revolutionary," which meant he was a domestic terrorist who caused a handful of issues. It was tradition for a prisoner to be released on a holy day, so during Passover, the public got to decide who walked free.

Pilate questioned and talked with Jesus and found no reason to charge Him. Three times Pilate attempted to exonerate Jesus and release Him, but the pressure from the Jews eventually caused Pilate to fold and give the people what they wanted. Pilate asks the crowd, "Do you want me to release … the King of Jews?" (John 18:39, CSB), and they shouted, "Not this man, but Barabbas!" (John 18:40, CSB).

How could they want to pardon a ruthless criminal? Barabbas made people's lives miserable. He murdered, lied, stole, and more. He was on death row for legitimate reasons. Jesus was only there because the Jewish religious leaders felt threatened by Him, and they did everything in their power to have him killed. Jesus was blameless. He healed the lame, brought sight to the blind, and resurrected the dead. How in the world did He become the guilty one? Jesus died the death that Barabbas deserved.

Jesus died the death we deserved.

Who is Barabbas? Barabbas is you and me.

All the sins we have committed and the judgment we deserve were settled once and for all on the cross. Our debt was paid in full by the One who knew no sin, but became sin so that we could become the righteousness of God (II Corinthians 5:21). God could not be just without the judgment of sin, so Jesus became that perfect sacrificial lamb on our behalf. *It is finished!* When we meet God at the end of this life, because of Jesus, we can meet Him face to face with anticipation and joy. That is the good news. Thank God for Jesus!

> But now the righteousness of God has been manifested
> apart from the law, although the Law and the Prophets bear
> witness to it—the righteousness of God through faith in
> Jesus Christ for all who believe. For there is no distinction:
> for all have sinned and fall short of the glory of God, and are
> justified by His grace as a gift, through the redemption that

is in Christ Jesus, whom God put forward as a propitiation by His blood, to be received by faith. This was to show God's righteousness, because in His divine forbearance He had passed over former sins. It was to show His righteousness at the present time, so that He might be just and the justifier of the one who has faith in Jesus.

Romans 3:21–26 (ESV)

CONCLUSION

For we are His creation, created in Christ Jesus
for good works, which God prepared ahead
of time so that we should walk in them.
Ephesians 2:10 (HCSB)

As I mentioned earlier in the book, if you would have told me that I would be writing a book, I would have surely laughed in your face. I struggled writing five-page, double-spaced papers in college, but clearly the Lord had other plans. This was challenging to write for a couple of reasons.

The first challenge came when I forgot the reason why I started to write in the first place. I noticed when I made this book about me, that is when I became anxious and doubtful. The thoughts that came to my mind were, "But what if it isn't good? What if no one buys it?" Literally, every negative "what if" came into my mind.

The Lord kept gently reminding me that He gave me an assignment to do for Him, not for me. When I reminded myself that it had nothing to do with me but only with the glory of God, that is when things began to come together. I had to continually ask myself if this book was for my kingdom or His. Yes, I want the book to flow when you read it, feel good in your hands, and be aesthetically pleasing. All those things are great, but the goal is to bring glory and attention to Him, not me.

Sadie Robertson Huff posted this on her Instagram one day, and it is exactly what I'm trying to say:

> There is no fear or pressure on you in building the Kingdom of God, but there is a lot of fear and pressure trying to build an empire for yourself.... It's not about being good enough, known enough, or even enough.... It's about the fact that God gave you life for such a time as this to be the light of the world.

The second challenge was the message I felt like the Lord wanted me to communicate. Don't get me wrong—I'm passionate about this topic. I think it is important for people to know what they believe, why they believe it, and if they even truly believe it. Although I'm passionate about it, it is not necessarily the message that most people want to hear today. This isn't a book about how to become the best version of you, how to make a bunch of money, or how to grow your platform on social media. (Honestly, you don't want me to write a book of any of those topics.) On the contrary, this is a message that will most likely make you uncomfortable. A message that challenges you to examine and check your heart. Checking yourself usually is not the most enjoyable process, and I decided to write a whole book about it.

As I wrote, I imagined seeing you about to walk off of a bridge to your death, but right before you took the step, I tackled you and saved your life. You're bruised a little bit and in some pain, but I just saved you from death. That's how I feel writing this book. I would rather bruise you now than for you to die without a relationship with Jesus Christ. Now, I don't believe anything that I have written will save you, but I hope that the Lord uses it to stir your heart and challenge you ... and ultimately, He will save your heart and soul.

After reading this, how are you doing? I hope that you have been challenged and your heart has been soft and teachable, rather than prideful and defensive. I hope that if you have been claiming to know Jesus, but your life looks no different than the world, that you will repent. I hope that if you have been claiming Jesus and think your works are enough to save you, that you will repent. If you have been self-righteous, doing all the things that you know you should do, but you have no true genuine relationship with Jesus, that you will repent.

I promise I'm not telling you anything that I haven't already learned and repented of myself. I hope it doesn't sound harsh, but if it does, and you turn from your sins and put your trust in Jesus, I'm okay with your being a little upset with me.

Your Turn

What would **you** say if you died and God asked, "Why should I let you in?" My hope is that after reading this, you know the answer. When I first heard this question, I had no clue at what the answer was. I hadn't even thought of death much. And my answer had nothing to do with the sacrifice of Jesus on the cross.

My initial answer was all about the things that *I* had done for God, but honestly, I had done those things to make myself look good. I hope you are thinking about it differently now and pausing long enough to figure out what you believe.

Please take time to ask yourself if your life reflects what you say. At the end of this life, when we are face to face with the Creator, we will either hear, "Well done good and faithful servant" (Matthew 25:21, CSB), or "I never knew you. Depart from me," (Matthew 7:23, CSB).

I hope you haven't finished this book and now feel like you need to do more. Hopefully you have realized that you can't do anything to earn the Father's love or earn a spot in heaven. What you can do, though, is open your hands, let go of your idols, and accept the free gift of salvation from Jesus. What would you say?

> And you were dead in your trespasses and sins in which
> you previously walked according to the ways of this world,
> according to the ruler who exercises authority over the lower
> heavens, the spirit now working in the disobedient. We
> too all previously lived among them in our fleshly desires,
> carrying out the inclinations of our flesh and thoughts, and
> we were by nature children under wrath as the others were
> also. But God, who is rich in mercy, because of His great
> love that He had for us, made us alive with the Messiah even
> though we were dead in trespasses. You are saved by grace!
> Together with Christ Jesus, He also raised us up and seated
> us in the heavens, so that in the coming ages He might
> display the immeasurable riches of His grace through His
> kindness to us in Christ Jesus. For you are saved by grace
> through faith, and this is not from yourselves; it is God's
> gift— not from works, so that no one can boast. For we are
> His creation, created in Christ Jesus for good works, which
> God prepared ahead of time so that we should walk in them.
> Ephesians 2:1–10 (HCSB)

NOTES

1. Oxford Dictionary

2. Abdu Murray, Saving Truth (Grand Rapids, Michigan: Zondervan, 2018).

3. Jackie Hill Perry, *How Adam and Eve Jacked up Everything (Genesis 1–3),* Recorded at True Conference 2019 in Atlanta, Georgia, https://www.youtube.com/ watch?v=QWqAdElTf9k&t=1251s.

4. William Blake, *Jerusalem: The Emanation of the Giant Albion,* Public Domain.

5. Oxford Dictionary

6. *HCSB Study Bible* (Nashville, Tennessee: Holman Bible Publishers, 2010).

7. Hanson, Melanie. "Average Student Loan Debt" EducationData.org, last revised July 10, 2021, https://educationdata.org/average-student-loan-debt.